TIGER WOODS
A BIOGRAPHY FOR KIDS

Libby Hughes

Kid Genesis

Kid Genesis is an imprint of
Genesis Press, Inc.
315 Third Avenue North
Columbus, Mississippi 39701

Tiger Woods: A Biography For Kids

ISBN 1-58571-003-2

Set in Centaur

Manufactured in the United States of America

FIRST EDITION

Dedicated to my golfing son-in-law

Brian W. Jones

Tiger Woods

Augusta, Georgia, April 1997.

There was a slight winter chill in the air. The wind had a sting to it, but the day was sunny. This was the 61st Masters Golf Tournament.

A certain magic hangs over the Augusta National Golf Club. The beautiful, brightly colored azalea bushes rise out of the pine needles amid the pencil-thin pines. The trees paint reflections on the jade green ponds and cast long shadows across the velvet greens and long fairways. A parade of distinguished golfers has thrilled crowds at Augusta for sixty years. Veterans like Arnold Palmer and Jack Nicklaus have inspired standing ovations.

At 1:44 P.M. on Thursday, April 10, Nick Faldo, 1996 Masters winner, walked to the first tee outside the pre-Civil War clubhouse. Friendly clapping greeted him. Tiger Woods, 1996 U. S. Amateur winner, made his way through the spectators. Fluff Cowan, his caddie, followed him. There were also cheers and applause for Tiger. An estimated 250,000 spectators would attend this match for four days while 300 or more media people would cover the event, broadcasting to 44 million TV viewers worldwide.

Traditionally, the previous year's Masters winner was paired with the U. S. Amateur champion. Faldo and Woods were the pair to play in 1997. The starter stepped forward to announce Nick Faldo. The crowd applauded.

He swung first. While Tiger waited, he took note of the weather. A pressing wind flapped against his black trousers. He wore a dark gray vest over his short-sleeved striped shirt. A black Nike cap completed the outfit. Tiger's stomach was in knots. But no one knew it. His face showed nothing.

Now it was his turn. The starter announced his name, and there was a round of applause but then instant silence. With assurance, Tiger strode to the tee. After plugging his ball into the ground, Tiger focused on the fairway and his target. The steep roller-coaster fairway and its two yawning bunkers (sand traps) at the top stared dangerously back at Tiger. He took a practice swing and looked again at his target. The crowd held their breath as Tiger hit his opening drive, the first swing in the tournament that would make him a golf superstar.

* * *

The Masters, which is held annually in Augusta Georgia, is among the most prestigious golf events in the world. This legendary tournament was started by Bobby Jones, one of the best golfers in the United States in the 1920s. His friend, Clifford Roberts, helped him form and finance the Augusta National Club. Jones won every amateur championship here and abroad between the ages of 14 and 28. At the peak of his career, he retired to become a lawyer. But his legend has lived through the decades.

A Biography For Kids

Robert Tyre Jones, Jr. lived in Atlanta, Georgia, and wanted a golf course of his own to play on during the winter season. A friend told him about a special property of 365 acres in Augusta, less than two hours from Atlanta. Located in a valley, Augusta's weather was warmer in winter than in Atlanta's. The land had been bought by a Belgian baron, Louis Mathieu Edouard Berckmans, in 1857 and turned into a nursery. A double lane of 60 magnolia trees led up to an antebellum (built before the Civil War) manor house where the European family lived. These magnolias today have low-growing limbs that are almost the size of a hippopotamus's belly. When Bobby Jones was taken to a hill in 1930 to survey the property, he fell in love with the terrain and flowering trees. It would be perfect for his golf course. The property was bought for $70,000 and financing was produced from a core of backers.

Eventually, the Augusta National Golf Club was formed as an exclusive private club for white men. Scottish designer, Dr. Alister Mackenzie, made the original plans for the course. At every hole a different flowering tree or bush was planted, including white and pink dogwoods and pastel-colored azalea bushes. In the circle in front of the clubhouse, an outline of the United States was sculpted and filled with yellow pansies. The club opened in January 1933. The manor house was transformed into the clubhouse, which was expanded by wings on either side over the years. In 1934 the first tournament was held. In

1938 the tournament name became the Masters.

The club built cabins and a private house near the clubhouse for General Dwight D. Eisenhower and his family in 1953. He had been invited to become a member in 1948. Ike loved to play golf and bridge with his male friends at Augusta, and they all wore green jackets.

The Augusta National Golf Club was under a cloud of white exclusivity from 1934 until 1975, when Lee Elder, an African-American, was invited to play at the club. Elder was also later invited by the club to watch Tiger Woods play in 1997. Even today a non-member of any race or gender cannot enter the clubhouse or grounds without an invitation from a member. It remains a private men's club. Only during the practice and tournament days in April for the Masters can members of the public walk the grounds and watch the tournament by purchasing tickets. They are still barred from the clubhouse.

Despite the restrictions, the Masters Tournament has a sacred ring to it. The name of Bobby Jones is still spoken with reverence. Great golfers such as Ben Hogan, Byron Nelson, Sam Snead, Gene Sarazen, Arnold Palmer, and Jack Nicklaus come to play with a feeling of awe. The beauty of the course, decorated by a dazzling array of spring flowers, creates an atmosphere unlike any other course.

The fairways are long and narrow, while the greens are fast and uneven. The water hazards and bunkers present a minefield for the players. Every year the course is challenging. But, the course suits Tiger Woods' game. He drives long, and if his putting is accurate, his chances of winning are good.

* * *

Tiger Woods was the 21-year-old new golf wonder, formerly from Cypress, California, and now from Orlando, Florida. Here he was at Augusta National Golf Club for the famous Masters tournament. This was Tiger Woods' third time at the Masters. Twice before he had been an amateur and had not done well. This time he was a professional. Since he was a child, he had dreamed of winning the Masters. More importantly, he wanted to slip his arms into the famous green jacket, awarded to every Masters winner. For years he had visualized himself wearing that jacket.

The tournament was a major test for Tiger. Could he compete against the golf greats: Jack Nicklaus, Arnold Palmer, Nick Faldo, Tom Watson, and others? Yes, he could. Since Monday, Tiger had been practicing. He had been relaxed but was still nervous. His parents, Earl and Tida Woods, were there, too. His father was recovering from heart trouble and couldn't walk the course to watch his son. Instead he sat near the 18th hole, watching Tiger on a television monitor. Tida followed Tiger discreetly from hole to hole.

Those first nine holes were a disaster. His score ended

in 40—not good for young Tiger, and he knew it. On the 10th hole he made a birdie (one stroke under par). At last he began to relax. For the second nine holes, he made 30, bringing the day's total to 70 and putting him in fourth place. Still, he was not pleased. Instead of retreating to the private house rented for him and his family, he headed to the driving range. "I came here to win," Tiger had told the press on Tuesday. He had to work on his swing and his shots if he wanted to achieve his goal. When dusk closed over him, Tiger returned home for dinner and to discuss the day with his dad, his coach, and a team of helpers.

That was the end of his first day of play. He had three more days to go, a total of four days and 72 holes—that was the same for every major tournament. Over four days the players would walk 25 miles across the less than 7,000 yards of the 18 holes. The course was beautiful but difficult.

Friday, April 11, would be a better day for Tiger. He was rested and had figured out what he needed to correct. This time he started in the afternoon at 2:29. He had eaten his bananas for energy as was his custom. His Nike outfit was blue and gray with a blue cap. The first nine holes produced a score of 34. When Tiger sunk a putt for eagle (two strokes under par) on the 13th hole, his mental game was working. He felt good and socked the air with a winning punch. The day's score totaled 66. Tiger was in first place.

But Tiger took nothing for granted. He left the 18th hole for the driving range and swung through two buckets of balls.

Saturday, April 12, was rainy. The sunshine and flowers were a blur; reflections on Ike's Pond were shattered by raindrops. The tall Georgia pines and open-jawed sand traps were still there. Tiger and his newly inherited caddie, Mike "Fluff" Cowan, headed for the first tee shortly after 2:00 P.M.

Cowan turned out to be one of Tiger's biggest assets during his first two years as his caddie. The Maine native, now living in Columbus, Ohio, not only was a pro-golfer himself in 1971, but he had caddied for 40 players over a period of 20 years. Approaching the age of 50 when Tiger hired him, his trademark was a white, walrus-style mustache. His experience and knowledge of golf courses across the country and abroad have been invaluable to his players. Before Fluff was hired by Tiger in August of 1996, he was Peter Jacobsen's caddie. His nickname comes from former U.S. Amateur champion, Steve Melnyk, who was the original "Fluff." Mike looked just like Steve and inherited his name.

Fluff could read weather changes and wind currents while on the golf course and helped Tiger determine what club to use. Tiger always made his own decisions, but Fluff offered a suggestion when asked. He also knew the bumps and breaks on the greens. Tiger credited him with many of his successes on tour. They were a balanced team. Fluff made ten percent of Tiger's earnings and $1,000 a week—handsome wages for a caddie.

Tiger was now paired with the Scottish golfer Colin Montgomerie. On this day Tiger wore a black-and-white striped shirt, off-white pants, and a black Nike hat. His beginning play was up and down. Disgusted with a bad putt, Tiger took off his hat and hit his leg. However, he shot 32 on the first nine and 33 on the back nine. Every once in a while he would give a half smile and a half wave to the clapping gallery. Now he was 15 under par and in the lead.

Sunday April 13, 1997, would be the biggest day in Tiger's professional life. The day was bathed in beautiful Georgia sunshine. Tee time would be a little after 3:00 P.M. for Tiger and Costantino Rocca. Suspense was building and excitement filled the air. The gallery was growing. Crowds necklaced every hole. The roars and groans and cheers grew louder. The course had a magical feel to it.

Tiger strode to the first tee with confidence. His face was emotionless. A slight wind rustled his black trousers. He wore a red shirt, which his mother believed was a winning color for him. His drive was long and straight. At the end of every swing, Tiger's body ended in an arched bow, with the club wrapped neatly behind his shoulders. His hips turned in perfect rhythm like that of a dancer.

As he approached the 18th green, he was 18 strokes under par and 12 strokes ahead of the runner-up, Tom Kite. Now he flashed his bashful smile, but maintained his concentration. Before Tiger reached the green for his final putts, a journalist asked Earl Woods what he felt at that moment. "The emotion of pride. Pride. Truly magnificent. A culmination of hard work—years and years of training and dreams. All coming to reality."

Tiger told himself, "This is a tough putt. Keep your focus." He was down to the final putt. Hundreds circled the green. The club's waiters and grounds crew stood in the background watching and cheering. A silence fell over the crowd. Tiger stroked his final putt. It rolled and rolled and missed. A sour groan escaped from the crowd. He had a four-foot putt left. Again, silence. He tapped the ball and dropped it into the little hole. Screams, whistles, wild applause erupted from the gallery. With a score of 270, Tiger Woods had won the 61st Masters tournament. He was the first non-white and the youngest player to achieve that honor. He struck the Georgia air with a series of uppercuts. Fluff was smiling broadly. Tiger hugged him.

As Tiger walked toward the clubhouse, Earl Woods stood ready to embrace the son who had earned his way from playing junior competitions to winning this event. Tiger wept in his father's arms, holding tight. They had embraced after the three junior championships, the three amateur wins, and now this one as a professional. Millions of television viewers who had never watched golf before cried with them. President Bill Clinton called this shot—the shot of Tiger hugging his father—the best of the week. Here was a true bond between father and son. Then,

Tida Woods joined the embrace. Yes, they had won. It took the three of them to win after all those years. Earl's predictions about his son had come true.

Then, it was time for Tiger to be the proud owner of that green jacket. Nick Faldo, the 1996 winner, held the jacket for Tiger. Someone handed Tiger a microphone. He thanked the black golfers who had blazed the trail for him, fighting racial prejudice. African-Americans like Lee Elder, Charlie Sifford, and Ted Rhodes had made it possible for him to play in the PGA Tour and at the Masters.

He paused and then told the world what his father had said to him the night before the final day, "'Son, this will be one of the toughest rounds of your life. If you just go out there and be yourself, it will be one of the most rewarding rounds in your life.' And he was right." That night, Tiger Woods slept holding on to his green jacket.

The engaging Tiger Woods became an instant celebrity. Every television network wanted to interview him. He landed on the cover of many magazines. "Tigermania" captured the imagination of people all over the world. Golf would never be the same as this Asian-African-American, who described himself as "Cablinasian" (*Ca* for Caucasian; *bl* for black; *in* for Indian; Asian), embarked on his professional career.

CHAPTER TWO: SOME HISTORY

A standard game of golf has 18 holes. Each hole starts at a tee and ends in a 4 1/4-inch cup sunk in a hole on the green. The object is to hit the ball into the cup in the least number of shots. The winner of each hole has the honor of driving first off the next tee. The person with the lowest number of strokes wins the game. Usually a par course can be finished in 70 or 72 strokes. There are 14 clubs in a golf bag, used for different kinds of shots.

The game of golf arrived in Scotland in the 15th century. Some sources speculate that it began in Germany even earlier. The players referred to the course as "links" because one hole was connected to another. Gradually they became known as golf links.

Golf clubs were made of hickory wood, and leather balls were filled with feathers. Eventually, the clubs evolved, and most now have steel and titanium shafts, while today's small white dimpled balls are composed of a synthetic cover over elastic and a liquid center. To brace themselves against the wind and cold of Scotland, the golfers wore knickers and long woolen socks, sweaters, and woolen caps. Today most golfers wear long trousers, colorful sports shirts, vests, and baseball type caps. There is greater freedom in the dress code. The Royal and Ancient Club of St. Andrews in Scotland (formed in 1754) has been revered for centuries. Tiger Woods has admitted his pleasure in playing that and other courses in Europe, allowing him more creativity in his game.

The first permanent golf club was organized in the United States in 1888. On January 1, 1898, a group of professional golfers played 36 holes at the Ocean County Hunt and Country Club in Lakewood, New Jersey. They played to win $150. The USGA (United States Golf Association) was formed in 1894. The PGA (the Professional Golfers' Association) was founded in 1916. In 1968, the PGA of America and the PGA Tour separated.

Until 1961 the PGA of America had a rule by which only members of the Caucasian race were allowed to play golf on PGA courses. Once that was changed, courses hosting tournaments changed the term "Open" to "Invitational" if they did not want non-whites to play at their events. By 1975 a few non-whites were playing professionally on the PGA Tour. However, racial prejudice lingered as late as 1990 in Birmingham, Alabama, but that was quickly changed when they hosted a PGA event. Such landmarks made it easier for Tiger to make his Masters' win in 1997. In some private country clubs, racial prejudice still exists, but in the professional ranks, a player cannot be rejected on the basis of race.

CHAPTER THREE: POP AND LITTLE MOMMY

Under the Georgia skies in April 1997, a new star was born whose fame would reach far beyond the world of golf and who would attract millions more fans to the game. Who was he? What were his secrets? How did it all start for the 6-foot 2-inch Tiger Woods?

Tiger's parents—they were the key. They helped shape his character. They influenced his attitudes. But they did not give him his talent for golf. That was a natural gift. Earl Woods described it as "a God-given gift." Once his parents recognized this gift, they provided every opportunity for Tiger to develop his love of golf.

To understand Tiger is to know a little bit about his parents, "Pop" and "My Little Mommy" as Tiger calls them. Mr. and Mrs. Earl Woods came from two different cultures and two different continents. Mr. Woods came from Kansas, in middle America, while Mrs. Woods grew up in the mystical country of Thailand, in southeast Asia.

Acres of wheat fields stretch across the state of Kansas. Sometimes the clouds almost touch the ripening grains as they bend with the breezes. The winds are constantly blowing. They whisper quietly during summer and whine loudly in winter. Kansas also has rolling hills, rivers, and lakes. Tiger's father grew up in the northeast corner of the state. The small city of Manhattan, Kansas, was home to Earl Woods, his brother, and four sisters. Manhattan was nicknamed the "Little Apple" after New York City's nickname, the "Big Apple." Earl Woods is an African-American, but he is also part American Indian, Chinese, and Caucasian.

Even though Earl's parents had died by the time he was 13, they had taught him special values that stayed with him during the years his sister, Hattie, raised him. His father encouraged him to play baseball. But his college-educated mother stressed the need for a good education. Earl followed his mother's influence by attending Kansas State University, located in the heart of Manhattan.

Attending the university on scholarship, Earl Woods earned all-state honors by playing catcher on the school's baseball team. Earl was the first black player to participate in the Big Seven (not the Big Eight) Conference of college baseball teams. While he was a student, he coached Little League all-star teams. In this "share and care" philosophy, which came from Earl's mother, Maude, one can see similarities between Earl and Tiger.

Earl's baseball talent was exceptional. In those days, however, the color of his skin barred him from being accepted into professional baseball. But he had the opportunity to join the Negro League baseball team after his freshman year. He turned down that offer to finish college as his mother wished. He hoped to become a teacher after graduating.

Since 1948, the United States Army has had a policy of nondiscrimination against African-Americans. Because Earl married his first wife at the young age of 21 and soon had three children to support, he joined the Army. Army wages were much better than those of a teacher. But his teaching skills became useful in the Army when he taught military history, tactics, and war games at City College of New York. He also trained as a Green Beret, one of the special forces of the army that requires extreme toughness and intelligence of its members.

Because of these qualifications as a Green Beret, Earl Woods served in the Vietnam War for two tours of duty in the 1960s, leaving his family behind. The tiny country of Vietnam, in Southeast Asia, was divided into South Vietnam and North Vietnam. The communist leaders of North Vietnam were determined to take over South Vietnam and unite the two countries into one communist nation. However, South Vietnam wanted to remain an independent country. Its leaders asked the United States to help them. In the beginning, Americans from various branches of the armed services were sent as advisers to train the South Vietnamese troops to resist the attacks of the North Vietnamese and Vietcong. Lieutenant Colonel Earl Woods was one of those advisers.

The jungles of Vietnam were dense and tangled. The climate was hot and oppressively humid—like Kansas in July and August. Earl was paired with a South Vietnamese Lieutenant Colonel Nguyen Phong on the battlefield and on the tennis court. They became like brothers. The enemy was often hidden, so Phong's eyes darted every-where to protect his men. He saved Earl from a sniper's bullet and from a poisonous snake that came close to biting him. From that time onward, Earl called Phong "Tiger" and vowed that if he ever had another son, he would call him Tiger in honor of Phong's courage and strength.

A few months before Earl left Vietnam, he and his first wife divorced. Their long separations during his time in the Army had changed their relationship. Earl was transferred to Bangkok, Thailand, not far from Vietnam. Thailand is a country of palaces, golden temples, statues of Buddha, rivers, and khlongs (narrow canals). The name of the country means "land of the free." The country is shaped liked the head of an elephant with its long trunk, reaching down into the Gulf of Thailand and bordering Malaysia. It is wedged between Laos, Cambodia, and Burma while its coastline rests along the Gulf of Thailand between the jade-green waters of the South China Sea and the Indian Ocean. Flowers and fresh fruits grow in abundance.

The Thai people are slender and charming. The country is a constitutional monarchy. Bangkok is a modern, bustling city along the Chao Phraya River. More than six million people live there. Like the city of Los Angeles, the Thai name for Bangkok means "City of Angels." Outside of Bangkok, life is very rural. Water buffaloes plow through the rice paddies and elephants lift sawed logs of teakwood with their trunks. Pleasant sounds of gongs, flutes, and xylophones fill the air.

Earl Woods found the charm and liveliness of Bangkok a welcome change from the strains of war he felt in Vietnam. He was an information officer for the Army in Bangkok. There his eye was caught by a very attractive young Thai woman working as a secretary in the U.S. Army office. Her name was Kultida Punsawad, Tida for short. Tida was mostly Thai, but she also had Chinese and Caucasian ancestry.

Earl and Tida quickly fell in love. When Earl was transferred back to the United States, to Fort Hamilton in Brooklyn, New York, he asked Tida to go with him. She did, and they were married there in 1969.

Shortly before Earl retired from the Army, a fellow officer invited him to play golf. This was a game Earl had never played. Because Earl considered himself a good athlete, he was dejected and humiliated when he was badly beaten. For the next four months, he practiced every day at the Army base's driving range. Then he challenged his friend to another round of golf at the course in Fort Dix, New Jersey. This time he beat his friend by four strokes and discovered that he was hooked on golf. If ever he had another child, Earl was going to introduce him to golf at an early age.

Finally, Earl retired from the Army in 1975 and moved to California. He found a job at McDonnell Douglas, negotiating contracts for materials for the rocket program. He and Tida looked for a small house nearby his work. They settled in Cypress, California, in Orange County, only 35 miles southeast of Los Angeles. They found a comfortable two bedroom house on a corner lot in a middle-class, white neighborhood.

The Woods house on Teakwood Street was beige stucco, trimmed in dark brown with the front covered in fieldstone. When they moved in, Tida was pregnant, and unfortunately, they were met with racial prejudice. No minorities lived in that white neighborhood in the 1970s. Their home was showered with limes and BB-gun shots. Earl and Tida refused to react or move out of the neighborhood, and when the neighbors realized the new family was going to stay, they stopped the attacks.

On December 30, 1975, Tida and Earl were blessed by the birth of their only child—a son. This child would combine the two cultures of his parents—Asian and African-American. Never believing that at the age of 44 he would have another son, Earl was especially happy. Earl wanted to name him Tiger in honor of his South Vietnamese friend, Nguyen Phong. But Tida wanted him to have a more formal name that represented the letters of their parents' names. Thus, the name Eldrick was formed and appeared on Tiger's birth certificate. Neither Tida nor Earl ever called the boy Eldrick, though. He was Tiger Woods from the start.

The family of three couldn't have been happier in their small house in Cypress. Tida watched over the baby with special care. In all of Tiger's childhood years, she never let a babysitter look after Tiger. If they were invited to a party, Earl went. Tida was a devoted mother and wife. Her child came first. She also was the disciplinarian. Tiger, in later years, described her as the one who set the rules in the house.

Earl established a close bond with his son from the moment he was born. At night, Earl would stand beside Tiger's crib and stroke his cheek. With his eyes closed, Tiger would smile. He knew his parents loved him. Earl admits that he was a much better father in middle age than he had been to his other three children. He blamed his earlier failure at fatherhood on his immaturity and youth. But he learned from his mistakes and spent much time with Tiger as a baby and beyond.

CHAPTER FOUR: A CHILD GENIUS

Earl's obsession with golf continued after Tiger was born. Near Cypress was the town of Los Alamitos where the Navy Destroyer Golf Course was located. Because of Earl's long association with the U.S. Army, he was allowed to play there. It was a flat, dry course with very few trees, but Earl loved the game. He turned his two car garage into a practice range. He put a carpet along the back wall and a net in front of it. Near the garage door, he had another carpet where he placed his golf balls and drove them into the net. He hit with each golf club again and again for hours, trying to perfect his swing.

When Tiger was six months old and could sit in his gray high chair with its red and white polka-dot flowers, Tida put him in the garage to watch his father. This was Tiger's entertainment for a couple of hours. His eyes never left his father and the ball. When Tida came out to feed him, Tiger refused. He wouldn't stop watching his father. So Earl and Tida devised a plan. Earl would make a shot and then stop. Tiger would turn his head to his mother, take a bite, and then turn back to his father. Hit, eat, hit, eat. That's how it went.

At the age of seven months, Tiger was given a little putter to have as a toy that he dragged in his round walker. By nine months of age, Tiger was walking. But he still liked to be strapped into his high chair to watch his daddy swing his golf clubs in the garage.

One day, Earl took a break and unstrapped Tiger from the high chair to let him toddle around the garage. Tiger waddled over to his little putter, picked it up, took a ball, and hit it perfectly into the net. Earl Woods was stunned, amazed, and speechless. He rushed into the house. "Tida, we have a child genius on our hands!" he exclaimed. Tida followed Earl back into the garage. With great excitement, Earl described how their baby son had grabbed his putter, copied Earl's little waggle before he swung his club, and hit the ball perfectly—swing and all. Tida was astonished. They looked at each other and knew that they did indeed have a child genius. They laughed, hugged each other, and hugged little Tiger. Whatever he had done, Tiger knew he had pleased his parents.

From then on, Earl Woods became a watchful caretaker in his mission to teach Tiger to play golf and to play it well. Tida was a participant, too. First of all, they decided not to ever push or force him to play golf. Tiger himself must want to practice and play. They wanted it to be fun—a game. They did not want to be stage parents, making their child successful for their benefit.

Around the house, little Tiger took the vacuum hose and hit a tennis ball up and down their hallway. He ignored his other toys in favor of the vacuum hose and putter. Already, golf was becoming as important to him as to his father.

When Tiger was 18 months old, his father took him to the driving range at the Navy Destroyer Golf Course.

TIGER WOODS

With Tiger in diapers, they began to practice pitching and putting. Pitch shots are those hit a short distance from the green. A number nine iron or a wedge iron can be used. The shot is intended to land as close to the cup as possible. Earl had Tiger pitch many balls from different places around the green. Then they would go onto the green and practice putting at different distances on the green, trying to sink each putt into the cup.

Earl had a few clubs cut down in size for Tiger. Because the short game (pitching and putting) is the most important in scoring points, Earl didn't teach Tiger to drive until he taught him the fundamentals of the short game.

A drive is made at the beginning of every hole. Between two markers, called the tee, a player sticks a little wooden peg in the ground and places a golf ball on it. He then swings a wooden driver or an iron club to hit, or drive, the ball as far down the fairway as he can. The drive is considered the easiest stroke. Tiger's hands were too small for the proper hand grip, so he used a baseball grip to give him power and strength.

By the time Tiger was two years old, he was very accomplished on the golf course. As a proud mother, Tida called a Los Angeles-based television station and invited the sportscaster to come see her little genius golfer perform. Although skeptical, the sports reporter went to the Navy Course to see Tiger. The reporter could not believe his eyes as he filmed the perfect golf strokes of this two-year-old. To his television viewers, the reporter said,

"This child will be to golf what Jimmy Connors and Chris Everett are to tennis."

Tiger's celebrity began at two years of age and has grown ever since. In fact, as a result of that story, talk show host Mike Douglas invited Tiger to appear with comedian Bob Hope and actor Jimmy Stewart for a game of putting. With his golf bag over his shoulder, Tiger climbed onstage to the makeshift putting green, but the carpet was uneven and he kept missing. After three failed attempts, Tiger picked up his golf ball and threw it into the cup. The audience roared with laughter as did Bob Hope and Mike Douglas.

At the age of two, Tiger entered a competition for boys ten and under on nine holes at the Navy Destroyer Golf Course and won. At the ripe old age of three, he entered a similar contest at the Naval course and won again, this time with a score of 48.

Another television program also wanted Tiger as a guest. After displaying his talent, Tiger sat on the host's knee and answered questions. The host asked him how he became so good at golf. Tiger replied, "Pwactice." How much practice was the next question. "A whole bunch," said Tiger. Then Tiger volunteered that he wanted to beat Jack Nicklaus and Tom Watson when he grew up. Tiger was three at the time. At the age of five, Tiger appeared on the popular "That's Incredible" TV show. So much attention was given Tiger, that Earl wanted to be sure he knew why he was special—because he had a gift, just like the other people on that TV show. He made sure Tiger understood that.

Earl Woods had long considered golf as a place to learn about life. It is a thinking game, and he wanted Tiger to learn how to think with each shot. Earl described to Oprah Winfrey on her television show in April 1997 how he prepared Tiger for this thought process at the age of three. He explained that he drew upon his military experience and shared it with Tiger. Earl applied the concept of Standard Operating Procedure (SOP) to Tiger's golf game. The idea of SOP is that through practice, an activity becomes routine and can be done well even under pressure. He told Tiger that the way to prepare for a golf shot is to get behind the ball first.

Tiger didn't like that. He didn't understand, and asked why. Earl answered by asking, "Doesn't every shot start with a target?" Tiger agreed.

"What better way to determine your target than to stand behind your ball and look at it," Earl said.

"You know, Daddy, that's right. That's a good idea," replied Tiger.

Next, Earl asked, "What do you have to know before you hit the ball?"

"How far I have to hit it, my distance," said Tiger.

"What else?"

"The wah wah (water) and the sand twap (trap)."

"What else?"

"If my ball's in a divot," said Tiger.

"That's called your lie," said Earl. "And there's something else."

Tiger couldn't think what it was until his father blew air to give him a hint. "Oh, the wind, Daddy. The wind."

All these points were part of the SOP that Earl was teaching Tiger, hoping they would become automatic in approaching every golf shot. Thought before action was the lesson—Earl made it fun and did it through questions and answers.

Eager to play golf, Tiger memorized his father's telephone number at work and from the age of two, he called his dad almost every day to ask if he could practice with him after work. Earl always paused after the question to keep his son in suspense and then he would say yes. Thrilled, Tiger would say that his mother would bring him to the golf course where they would meet. Before Tiger could read or write, he knew the golf terms and could figure out how each hole should be played.

Earl and Tiger experienced racism while they were playing on the Navy Destroyer Course. Whenever Earl and his son entered the clubhouse or cafe, there was silence. Earl asked if Tiger could play the course without adult supervision. He was refused, despite the fact that white youngsters were allowed to play without supervision. (The other parents may have been jealous that Tiger had won all the tournaments against their children.)

Tida began going to all the courses in the area to find one that would allow Tiger to play on his own. In Long

Beach, California, she found Heartwell Golf Park, a par-3 course. This was a shorter 18-hole course designed for the short game. It was a public course on busy Carson Boulevard and only ten miles from Cypress. Today Heartwell is still a very pretty course with rich green fairways, framed by palm, pine, willow, and oak trees.

At Heartwell, Tiger was introduced to a young and engaging golf pro, Rudy Duran. He agreed to let Tiger play once he saw Tiger's extraordinary golf talent. Duran became Tiger's golf instructor from the time Tiger was four until he was ten. Rudy is now a golf pro at Chalk Mountain School in Atascaderos, California. This is what he had to say about his first impressions of Tiger: "When I first saw him at four years old, it was unbelievable. There he was smacking balls like a pro. He was a genius like Einstein or Mozart. What he needed to know from me were the basic things about golf and the rules. Then, he needed to be reassured that he was doing everything correctly. When he was doing everything well, there was plenty of praise. When something wasn't right, I didn't criticize, but just gave him the right information, so that he could process the information and execute it. I gave him new information on specifics about his short game and putting. He was far superior to any other kid. He was amazing. I knew he was going to be a superstar from the beginning."

Soon it was time for Tiger to enter Kindergarten at the Cerritos Elementary School in Cypress. Because it was only a block and a half away from his home, Tiger could walk there easily.

Tiger's first day of school would be the worst of his life. At recess, some older white boys took Tiger to the Bartoldi/Sycamore Park near his house and tied him to a tree. They threw rocks at him and shouted racist names. Bleeding, Tiger ran home crying. Earl cried, too. But Tida kept her eyes dry. In her Thai culture it would be a loss of face to show tears.

The boys who beat up Tiger were punished for their behavior, and when Tiger returned to school as the only black child, he blended in with his classmates and there were no other incidents.

It was obvious that Tiger was very bright for his age. Tida had worked with him since he was two, showing him flash cards for words and math. His kindergarten teacher told his parents that Tiger could very easily skip a grade. Earl and Tida talked it over with Tiger, but he decided he wanted to stay with his own age group.

By the time Tiger was six, his father had discovered some cassette tapes that might help Tiger maintain his confidence and self-esteem. They were quite soothing and helpful. Young Tiger nearly wore them out and even wrote some of the messages on paper and attached them to his bedroom wall. Here are some of them:

I will my own destiny.

I believe in me.

I smile at obstacles.

My strength is great. I stick to it easily, naturally.
I focus and give it my all.
My decisions are strong. I do it all with my heart.

Tiger applied these sayings to his golf game at the Optimist Junior World international tournament at Presidio Hills in San Diego, California. In the ten and under class, the six-year-old placed eighth out of 150 entrants. At eight and nine years old he won that same tournament and repeated his win in an older division at the ages of twelve and thirteen. He swept the junior world of golf in southern California, winning 30 tournaments by 1987.

Rudy Duran often used six-year-old Tiger to help conduct clinics for kids. One time he took Tiger to Chaulk Mountain and asked him to execute many different shots. Tiger could do them on command—low, high, short, long. He also was able to analyze someone else's swing and explain what the flaws were. Another time, Rudy took Tiger (still age six) to an exhibition game with famous golfer Sam Snead. Tiger and Snead were to play two holes, the 17th and 18th, as competitors. On the seventeenth, a par 3, Tiger hit his first shot to the edge of the water in a terrible lie. Snead offered to let him hit another shot, but Tiger didn't. He went right up to his ball, figured out where he should hit it, and placed it on the green. In two putts his ball was in the cup, only one stroke behind Sam Snead. Snead and everyone else were amazed. Snead said, "I've worked for years to get the hitch out of that swing of mine and along comes this kid with a perfect swing. I think I'll toss my clubs in the lake some place."

From the time he was a toddler, Tiger displayed a natural talent for playing golf. His swing is nearly perfect. It has a beauty and grace unlike any other golfer. His hip speed is fast and sometimes gets ahead of his club head, causing the ball to hook or slice to the right or left. Because he can drive the ball over 300 yards, he has to exercise great control over the speed and strength of his swing. Once, in Colorado, he drove the ball 426 yards— an unbelievable distance.

His best performances have happened when he was behind in a tournament and had to fight his way back to gain the lead. He likes the challenge and competition in golf and considers it a thinking game. Spectators enjoy watching his style and technique even when he is just hitting balls from the driving range.

CHAPTER FIVE: SCHOOL FIRST, GOLF SECOND

Tida was deeply involved in Tiger's activities throughout his childhood. She drove her son to all the tournaments in the area. She always stayed in the background, cheering her son and his competitors when they made an excellent shot. She kept Tiger's scorecard at every tournament, and she insisted that Tiger show good sportsmanship to the winners and shake their hands.

When it came to discipline, Tiger's mother used a special weapon over him: His golf clubs. They were her weapon for discipline. Tiger had to do his homework or he could not practice or play golf. That was the rule. And he obeyed, not only out of respect for his parents, but because he wanted to play golf more than anything.

A majority of parents in Asia consider education the highest goal. Earl agreed with Tida because his own mother had told him how important education is in life. Education came first.

Tida had always wanted to introduce Tiger to his Asian heritage, so when he was nine years old, she and Tiger flew to Thailand to meet relatives and see the beauty of the land and its people. She took with her a special chart about Tiger she had kept from the moment of his birth. Keeping such a chart was a Buddhist tradition. (Tida had been raised in the Buddhist religion, which began with an Indian philosopher 2,500 years ago.) She took Tiger's chart to a Buddhist monk in Bangkok. The monk knew nothing about Tiger, but the chart amazed him. He said this was a very special child like an angel from God and that he would be a successful leader in whatever did, such as becoming a great general. Now Tida knew for sure that her son was going to do great things in golf or perhaps something else.

When they returned to United States, Tiger made a chart that he put on the wall in his room. This chart showed all the achievements Jack Nicklaus had made from a young adult to the present. Tiger contrasted his own achievements alongside Nicklaus's, and Tiger had outscored Nicklaus in most of them. Tiger dreamed of playing and beating all the great golfers.

As Tiger grew older, Tida was concerned about his thick glasses and rather toothy smile. She wanted him to wear contact lenses and be fitted with braces. He resisted the contact lenses and refused to open his eyes at first when they were inserted. In moments, however, he opened his eyes and could see perfectly and comfortably. He has worn them ever since. Although the braces for his teeth cost $4,000, they have given him a "million dollar smile."

At the age of ten, Tiger told his parents he wanted to go to college to study accounting. They couldn't understand why until he said that he wanted to learn how to manage the money that he would earn. Earl and Tida were astonished. Later Tiger asked his father in all seriousness if Earl could live on $100,000 a year. Amused, Earl said he'd like to think about that more deeply. Tiger was a man in a child's body.

Once Tiger completed elementary school, he moved to the Orangeview Middle School in Anaheim. Although it was less than a mile away, it was not in Cypress, but it was part of the school district for Cypress residents. Along wide Orange Avenue were mimosa trees with peach-colored blossoms and pale pink oleander bushes. Behind these trees was the white one-story school, trimmed in sky-blue. On the school grounds were charming oaks and dense clusters of red bougainvillea. Because of the warm weather in California, picnic tables were outside for lunch periods.

Tiger's seventh and eighth-grade history teacher, Carl Vanderbosch, has commented that Tiger "was an excellent student—as mature as a college student. He was involved in class and asked questions. One day in early spring, he came into class excited and told me his handicap was down to one. I put him in the gifted class in eighth grade. He was attentive and never in trouble. He didn't miss school. He made up the work if he was away on a trip. He didn't have an attitude, but was easy going and had his work in on time. He wasn't self-centered. I remember he went out for the basketball team. When we were studying Asian religions, he volunteered that he was a Buddhist. I would think just as highly of him even if he had never hit a golfball."

Upon Tida's advice, Tiger began to use his clubs as a "weapon" against racial prejudice. At a golf tournament in southern California, Tiger missed a shot and flipped his

Tiger at age four with his first coach, Rudy Duran.

The house in Cypress, California where Tiger grew up. The garage is where he swung his first golf club at the age of 9 months.

Tiger attended Cerritos Elementary School in Cypress, California.

The outdoor cafeteria at Orangeview Middle School in Anaheim, California where Tiger was a student.

Tiger with the other members of the Western High School golf team. Coach Don Crosby is on the far right.

Stanford University, where Tiger studied accounting for two years before turning pro.

Butch Harmon, Tiger's coach, at the 1998 Masters.

Tiger watches his partner pitch to the green the day
before the start of the 1998 Masters.

club in the air. It fell to the ground accidentally. In junior golf, a player can be disqualified for throwing a club in a fit of anger. Two white youngsters reported Tiger to the authorities and he was disqualified. As Tiger and Tida drove home, Tida told Tiger not to get angry, not to get revenge on those boys, but to let his clubs speak for him. In other words, with his clubs he could win tournaments. What greater weapon is there than winning with his golf clubs.

Unfortunately Tiger's golf coach, Rudy Duran, took a new job far from Long Beach, and Tiger had to find a new teacher. Earl and Tiger approached John Anselmo, the golf pro at the Meadowlark Public Golf Course in Huntington Beach. Tiger would study with the quiet, unassuming Anselmo from ages 10 to 18 and change the plane of his swing.

The Meadowlark course faces the long, sandy string of Huntington Beach on the coast of the Pacific Ocean. From the driving range, each shot seems to reach for the waves. The two-story club house is like a Spanish villa, with its arches and red tiled roof that overlook the course, studded with sturdy live-oak trees. Here, not far from Cypress, Tiger practiced against the sea breezes under Anselmo's guidance.

In an interview, Anselmo said about Tiger: "He was an exciting young man to watch and did everything well. When he was young, he was quiet, always thinking. In his teens, he became more outgoing. I never saw him show any emotion until he won his first U. S. Amateur championship. When I was teaching him, we had to work on his growing into his golf swing through working on different shots. From the beginning he was competitive—even more so in high school. His most outstanding quality is intelligence, and I found him always gracious. He will do a lot in life."

At the age of 13, Tiger was already gently being recruited by colleges and universities such as Stanford, the University of Nevada, and Arizona State University. They were eager to have such a talent on their golf teams. Tom Sargent, a golf pro at Yorba Linda Country Club, had watched Tiger in the junior tournaments since Tiger was nine and was impressed. Sargent was highly respected and was named National Golf Pro of 1997 by the PGA. When Tiger was ten or eleven, Sargent wrote to the golf coaches at these universities, asking them to keep this talented young golfer in their memory banks.

Sargent said in an interview: "He was mature for his age—seemed older than his peers and more focused. He was patient and not impetuous, but had the fire inside. Like any golfer, he gets angry at himself when he misses a shot, but he puts the anger behind him and handles the reaction. When Tiger was 14 and 15 years old, I had to introduce him at the awards ceremonies, and I said he was the best in the world. Every year he was the best player in the world. Nobody has done what he has. Somehow Tiger was able to separate his golf celebrity from his school life and home life. He is bringing people out to watch golf who have never played golf or even been interested in the game. It will change golf and have a positive effect."

Sargent added this comment: "Everybody expects Tiger to win, but he will play to *his* expectations. He is his own person. The greatest gift his parents gave him was to let him make his own decisions. I never saw Earl tell him to do this or that. He makes his choices and lives by his standards. He is the best."

As a result of Sargent's suggestion to Stanford University to consider Tiger in the future, a letter arrived for Tiger when he was 13. It was from the golf coach, Wally Goodwin, indicating that Stanford might be interested in him. Without any help from his parents, Tiger replied to the coach's letter. So impressive was the letter that Goodwin gave a copy to some members of the Stanford golf team. The punctuation, grammar, and sentence structure were perfect.

Dear Coach Goodwin,

Thank you for your recent letter expressing Stanford's interest in me as a future student and golfer. At first it was hard for me to understand why a university like Stanford was interested in a thirteen-year-old seventh grader. But after talking with my father I have come to better understand and appreciate the honor you have given me. I further appreciate Mr. Sargent's interest in my future development by recommending me to you.

I became interested in Stanford's academics while watching the Olympics and Debbie Thomas. My goal is to obtain a quality business education. Your guidelines will be most helpful in preparing me for college life. My GPA this year is 3.86 and I plan to keep it there or higher when I enter high school.

I am working on an exercise program to increase my strength. My April USGA (United States Golf Association) handicap is 1 and I plan to play in SCPGA (Southern California Professional Golf Association) and maybe some AJGA (American Junior Golf Association) tournaments this summer. My goal is to win the Junior World in July for the fourth time and to become the first player to win each age bracket. Ultimately, I would like to be a PGA professional. Next February I plan to go to Thailand and play in the Thai Open as an amateur.

I've heard a lot about your golf course and I would like to play it with my dad some time in the future.

Hope to hear from you soon.

Sincerely,
Tiger Woods 5-5/100 (His height and weight.)

To earn a scholarship to Stanford, Tiger had to be more than an exceptional golfer; his grades had to be an average of A or A-. Academically Stanford is very hard, and only the best students are accepted. So Tiger had to keep his golf and his course work at a high level of excellence. This left very little time for a social life. Once a girl asked him out when he was in eighth grade, and he had to politely explain that he was too busy with golf.

At one point, when Tiger was 13, he went to his father and asked him to prepare him for the toughness he needed in playing golf. Earl accepted. Drawing from his years of training as an Army Green Beret, Earl put his son through a tough program. On the golf course, Earl jingled his keys or dropped them just as Tiger was about to drive his ball. He coughed. He moved as Tiger was putting. He said terrible things to him such as, "Watch out you don't hook that shot." Although Tiger bristled, he knew this was what he wanted his dad to do—all the things that his opponents might do to make him lose his focus—and it helped him develop a coldness to protect himself from such tricks.

Also helping with his mental toughness was a Navy Captain, Dr. Jay Brunza, who was a clinical sports psychologist. He played on the Navy course and had come to know Earl and Tiger. He joined what became known as the "Tiger Team." He, too, helped Tiger keep his focus under stressful conditions in tournament play. Brunza sometimes caddied for Tiger during junior tournaments.

Earl always encouraged Tiger to play golf for his own pleasure and not try to please anyone but himself. Earl didn't want Tiger to play golf or hit a shot just to please his father. Even when Tiger didn't win, Earl was always proud of him and never criticized him. Tida, on the other hand, was more passionate and wanted Tiger to "kill" his opponents, despite her desire to have him be sportsman-like. However, one thing Earl would not tolerate was moodiness, sulking, or quitting on the golf course. If Tiger didn't like one of his shots, he had to forget it and move on.

Once, in a special tournament, Tiger forgot this rule. He quit. At the end of the tournament and in private, Earl gave him a tough lecture. His desire for Tiger was to be a good person first and a good golfer second. These were always Earl's priorities.

One of Earl's goals was to retire early to take over Tida's role and travel with Tiger to golf tournaments all over the country. In 1988, when Tiger was twelve, Earl did retire and Tida went to work. The Woods were spending $20,000 a year on golf lessons, golf clubs, entry fees, food, and travel. Their house had a second mortgage, and they were stretched financially beyond their limits. But the trophies Tiger was winning filled the house and garage, and his parents never regretted spending the money on their son.

As a normal teenager, one of Tiger's passions off the golf course was eating junk food. He loved cheeseburgers, fries, and strawberry shakes and still does. Tacos and pizzas ranked high, too. But steaks were a special treat. For fun, he relished playing video games with his friends. Beating them helped satisfy his competitive instinct. He liked music. His dad had introduced him to jazz from the time he was in the crib, but rap and rock music can really move him as well. After graduating from Orangeview Middle School, Tiger took his next big jump.

Chapter Six: High School and College

Western High School in West Anaheim—that was the big time for Tiger. Just down the street from Orangeview, it was a place of glamour for the students at the middle school. They thought the big "W" in front and the building colors of dark blue and white were awesome. Here the mix of students was multicultural and multiracial. There were Mexicans, blacks, Asians, and whites. Some were from middle-class homes and some weren't, but the parents were interested in the school and how their children performed.

Someone at Western High had long been waiting for Tiger's arrival as a freshman. He was the golf coach, Don Crosby. The broadly-built Crosby had followed the young man's phenomenal golf career on the junior circuit. He couldn't wait to have Tiger on the school's golf team. On first impression, Crosby might appear gruff and tough, but he had a good heart and was an inspiring coach to young men and women. He cared about the kids on and off the course. Many confided in him as a friend.

Before his 31-year coaching stint at Western, he had taught football greats such as Terry Metcalf, David Wilson, and Todd Marinovich. Crosby also taught accounting, and Tiger became his teaching assistant during his junior year.

When Tiger arrived at Western as a freshman, his physique was very much like a young Thai boy—medium-tall and very slender. According to Crosby, he was 5 feet

8 inches tall and weighed 130 pounds. But the reed-like teen was already one of the best junior players. Crosby had seen him at the Yorba Linda Country Club where Tom Sargent declared Tiger the best in the world. Skeptical, Crosby watched Tiger play 18 holes and was won over to Sargent's viewpoint. Crosby wanted to start a Junior Varsity team at Western to use Tiger's talents.

Crosby said in an interview: "Tiger was quiet as a freshman. Like any other kid who wanted to go to Stanford, Tiger knew what he wanted and knew what he needed to do over four years to get there without distractions—such as girls or drugs. He stayed focused. Academics came first with Tiger. He loved to practice, but his mother insisted on homework first. He kept his grades high all four years and made the National Honor Society. Tiger had honesty, integrity. He was an athlete and a scholar. He could have asked for favors, but he never did. He loved the competition in the classroom and wanted to make the highest grade."

In between school and golf competitions, Tiger and his father continued to hold golf clinics for inner-city kids around Los Angeles. Again, this was part of the "care and share" belief that Earl had learned from his mother and was now passing on to his son. One time they went into the heart of Los Angeles where gangs were a fact of life. Two rival gangs agreed to put aside their fighting to attend Tiger's clinic. Already Tiger was achieving what Earl had wished for—a mission that went beyond golf. In these sessions, Tiger demonstrated how he couldn't hit the ball correctly if he were taking drugs. Although the kids laughed, he made his point.

Because Western didn't have a golf course, the team had to practice on public courses nearby. Crosby discovered the courses were far too easy for Tiger. Besides, Tiger had won the CIF (California Interscholastic Federation) title and the SCGA (Southern California Golf Association) title in his freshman year. Tiger needed a bigger challenge. With the support of Principal Craig Haugen, Crosby begged the owner of the private Los Coyotes Country Club in Buena Park to let the high-school team practice on their course. He agreed. It was a hard course, and Tiger benefited from the challenge.

In his sophomore year, Tiger took the honors chemistry course taught by Corina Durrego, a slim, attractive teacher who had the reputation of being a hard grader. In an interview in a Western High School classroom, she said, "He was a genuine person with real talent. A regular kid. He got a B in my class, but I'm a hard grader. He was good in math. I asked him what he wanted to be when he grew up, and when he said an accountant, I wanted to know why. 'To keep track of the money I'm going to make and the people who will manage it,' was his reply."

During his sophomore year, Tiger's golf wins were not quite as spectacular. He missed winning both the CIF and SCGA titles. But in his junior and senior years he won the CIF title again. His grades continued to climb and in his junior year, Tiger had a 4.0 average.

Tiger's life was not all school and golf. For fun he played basketball, went bike riding, worked out in the gym, and played video games, especially "Mortal Kombat." He liked to play with his two dogs, Joey (a yellow lab) and Penny (a mixed breed). He had a girlfriend and liked to go to parties. His best friend was Bryon Bell, who played on the golf team also. Bryon was tall, handsome, lanky, quiet, and very smart. He planned to become a doctor and attended the University of California at San Diego after graduating from Western. It was understood that he would become Tiger's doctor in the future.

Meanwhile, Tiger was entering professional tournaments as an amateur. His trophies and awards were growing. He was playing with some of the best players on the PGA tour—Greg Norman, John Daly, and Mark O'Meara—and nearly beating them. In West Los Angeles at a clinic, Jack Nicklaus saw him swing and said to Tiger, "When I grow up, I want to have a swing as pretty as yours." In the spring before graduating, he returned to Thailand to play in the Johnnie Walker Asian Classic. Although he tied for 34th, his Thai fans flocked to the tournament in record numbers to watch their "native son."

Some exclusive country clubs were offering Tiger honorary memberships to play on their courses. One of these was the Big Canyon Country Club in Newport Beach, California, where the fee to enter is usually $100,000. But some Southern golf courses still excluded blacks from membership and from playing on their courses. The private and exclusive Shoal Creek Country Club in Birmingham, Alabama, was one of these. When Shoal Creek was hosting a PGA tournament in 1990, their policy of not allowing blacks into membership was uncovered through an interview with Hall Thompson, its president. A huge controversy exploded in the nationwide press. The PGA threatened to remove the tournament unless blacks were allowed. The tightly guarded club, behind tall wrought iron gates and a guardhouse, quickly admitted a respected black advertising executive, Louis Willey, to honorary membership. The controversy was resolved and the PGA tournament proceeded. But the incident left deep scars on Thompson. Only a few other blacks have been admitted since then. At the time this happened, Tiger was 14. When he was told about it, he made no comment but went out on a California course the next day and finished with a score of 66—a very low score for 18 holes.

When Tiger was on the Stanford golf team, he did play on Shoal Creek, winning for his team. Some African-Americans in Birmingham protested outside the gates of Shoal Creek, urging the Stanford team and Tiger not to play because of the Club's anti-black policies. Tiger and coach Wally Goodwin rejected that plea. In fact, Hall Thompson congratulated Tiger on being an outstanding golfer. Tiger preferred to follow his mother's advice to him years before to meet racial opposition through his talent—letting his golf clubs speak for him.

Before graduating with honors from Western High School, Tiger would be named Southern California Player of the Year at age 14; youngest player to win U.S. Junior National Championship at 15, tapped as Player of the Year by *Golf Digest* at 15; first golfer to win U.S. Junior National Championship twice at 16, and named Titleist-GolfWeek National Amateur of the Year at 16. He would also win the USGA Junior National Championship for the third time at 17 and be named GolfWorld Player of the Year at 17.

For coach Don Crosby, probably the most exciting award that Tiger received was the Dial Corporation award as the top national high school male athlete. He and Tiger traveled together to Washington, D.C., for the banquet. They went sightseeing in the nation's capital and were photographed together under the Washington Monument.

Despite the many golf successes, Earl Woods could see that junior golf was too easy and was beginning to bore his son. When they were in Houston, Texas, for a U.S. Amateur tournament, Earl decided it was time that Tiger had a golf coach from the professional ranks. The famed Butch Harmon, who had coached Greg Norman and others, was the choice. Before moving to Las Vegas in 1997, Harmon was the golf pro at the exclusive men's Lochinvar Club in Houston. His father, Claude Harmon, had won the Masters in 1947. Harmon assessed Tiger's swing and game and thought it would take three years of working with Tiger to perfect it. Harmon was hired.

For college, Tiger had offers from Nevada and Arizona schools, but he chose Stanford University. The staff agreed to customize his courses to accommodate his golf scholarship. Driving his father's old Toyota, Tiger set off for Palo Alto, California, 250 miles north of Cypress, near San Francisco. Palo Alto is a typical college town, whose main street is lined with giant magnolia trees.

Nicknamed "The Farm," Stanford University sits on a parcel of 8,100 acres that once was a stock farm for cattle and horses. Leland Stanford had struck it rich during the California gold rush and bought the farm with his profits. When his fifteen-year-old son Leland Stanford, Jr. died in 1884, Stanford and his wife built the university as a memorial to him.

The long Palm Avenue, lined with sturdy palm trees, leads to the entrance of the Spanish-style buildings. The buildings spread like wings across the horizon. The tan walls and clay-tiled roofs seem more like a Spanish mission than a university. Behind the first flank of buildings is a broad quadrangle (an area surrounded on four sides by buildings or arcades) with arcades of arched walls. The second largest collection of Rodin sculptures in the world is arranged attractively on the Quad. Classrooms, offices, cafeteria, and special departments are all behind the Quad. Dormitories and fraternity and sorority houses stretch along one arm of the campus. The tower dominates the entire campus.

For his freshman year, Tiger was assigned to the Larkin Dormitory in Stern Hall. The two story dorms are an earthen beige and desert coral. Tiger was given a non-golfing roommate from West Virginia.

Even before freshman orientation, Tiger was spirited away with the Stanford Cardinals' golf team to play a tournament in New Mexico. Although the academics were harder and more challenging than at Western High School, Tiger loved college life. Here he could escape the media and fade into student life with 7,000 undergraduates. His peers were bright and had scored 1500 or higher on their SAT tests. To keep up, students stayed up late studying and talking.

Naturally, Tiger's favorite place was the Stanford golf course. Nestled in the foothills behind the main campus, the golf course has a distant view of San Francisco Bay. Tiger enjoyed playing on the rolling fairways framed by pines, willows, and oak trees.

Guided by the likable coach, Wally Goodwin, the golf-team members became Tiger's friends. They were amazed at Tiger's golfing skills. He could mimic the swings of all the best golfers. He could do trick shots like pretending to drive the ball at the dormitories and hooking it back onto the driving range.

His team members teased him, too. At night, Tiger would take out his contact lenses and put on his thick glasses. They called him Urkel—the nerdy kid on the TV comedy "Family Matters." He hated it. Casey Martin, who had a disabled leg, was a team friend who played practical jokes like telephoning Tiger and pretending to be a journalist interviewing him. Martin made news in 1997, when he won a court case giving him permission to use an electric cart on the PGA Tour.

Some of Tiger's teammates belonged to a fraternity, and Tiger soon became a pledge of the Sigma Chi Fraternity, a large two-story white house located near the main campus.

Tiger selected an IDM (Individually Designed Major) to meet the required courses and explore his own interests. He took African-American Studies as an introduction to history, literature, and culture within the American Culture. Only the countries of West Africa and South Africa were covered from the African continent. History, Computer Science, and golf were his other courses along with race and ethnicity and Portuguese Literature.

For his purposes, Tiger wanted to take accounting, but there were no undergraduate courses in accounting. However there was a small section in the graduate Business School (for Masters or Ph.D. candidates) for undergraduates. It was called the Poet's Corner. Here students learned the principles and concepts of financial reports, income statements, and financial positions. This was just what Tiger wanted for his future needs as a professional golfer.

Life on campus was not free of racial or violent incidents. Tiger was sometimes called racist names. One night he had been out and had come back to the Stern Hall parking lot around 11:00. As he headed toward his dorm, someone grabbed him from behind, wielding a knife. Calling him by name, the mugger demanded Tiger's wallet. Tiger had left it in his car. The mugger searched him. Then he ripped off his gold rope chain and took his watch. Usually, Tiger wore around his neck the 400-year-old Buddha charm given to him by his mother, but he didn't have it on that night. The thief dealt a final blow to his jaw and ran. Tiger called the campus police. He then phoned his father and told him about the episode, joking that his teeth were now perfectly aligned.

For his sophomore year, Tiger moved over to one of the four Suites Dormitories right next to the driving range. Since the range was open until 9:00 P.M., he could practice before studying.

During school sessions, Tiger entered collegiate tournaments. In the summers he played in the amateur tournaments. His awards and wins continued to build. He had already won three USGA Junior National Championships. By the end of his sophomore summer at Stanford, he had won three consecutive U.S. Amateur titles. He tied for 67th in the British Open at age 19 and rose to 22nd at age 20. In 1995 he tied for 41st at the Masters. Then, just before Tiger became a college junior, he made a dramatic decision.

Chapter Seven: Fame, Fortune, and the Future

From August 28, 1996, life would never be the same for Tiger Woods. He announced to the world that he would not return to Stanford but would become a full-time professional golfer. This was both shocking and not shocking. He wanted to finish college and earn a degree, mainly because he had promised his parents he would. But collegiate golf was no longer a challenge. His skills had reached the level of pros on the PGA Tour. Although he regretted leaving his Stanford friends and the joys of college life, this was the right time for him. Besides, he planned to complete his degree by correspondence courses for those last 90 units he needed. As yet, he has not finished, and Tiger Woods has joined other Stanford non-graduates like tennis star John MacEnroe, author John Steinbeck, actor Ted Danson, poet Robert Pinsky, and actor Fred Savage.

Events during the spring and summer of 1996 had helped to determine Tiger's decision. In the spring, Tiger returned to Augusta, Georgia, for his second time as an amateur. Jack Nicklaus, Arnold Palmer, and Tiger played a practice round together. Nicklaus and Palmer were amazed by Tiger's long drives and his short game. Nicklaus declared that Tiger would win more Masters tournaments than he and Palmer had won together (six for Nicklaus and four for Palmer). South African golfer Gary Player said that Tiger Woods was golf's next superstar. Unfortunately, to everyone's surprise, Tiger did not make the cut to play at the Masters in 1996. However, his celebrity was well established.

Also, he did not win at the U.S. Open in Michigan or the British Open in St. Andrew's, Scotland. However, he had placed 22nd at the British Open and was awarded a silver medal for top score as an amateur. Then, Tiger won his third consecutive U.S. Amateur Championship in Oregon. One championship he had not won was the NCAA (National Collegiate Athletic Association). Jack Nicklaus had won both in the same year. Tiger wanted to do the same. When the NCAA finals were played in Tennessee, Tiger won. At age 20 he had achieved all his amateur goals. He was ready for the pros. Butch Harmon thought he was ready, too. So did Earl.

As with Michael Jordan and other promising sports talents, agents had been swarming around Tiger since he was 14. They had a feeling he would become a famous golfer. Being Tiger's agent would make an agency wealthy. Earl started scouting for the right agency when Tiger was in his teens. Because Earl wanted international exposure for his son, he finally decided on IMG (International Management Group), headquartered in Cleveland, Ohio. Hughes Norton, head of the group, became very much impressed with Tiger's game and his winnings.

Such companies as Nike, Titleist, American Express, Rolex, and Warner Books were wooing Tiger to endorse their products. After he won his third U.S. Amateur title, on August 12, 1996, Nike's head, Phil Knight, was there.

He whisked Tiger and his family over to Nike's corporate tent for a celebration. Nike took the Woods family to Michigan in the company's private jet and suddenly Tiger Woods was a rich young man. Hughes Norton of IMG had negotiated a $40 million contract with Nike over five years and a $20 million contract with Titleist over five years. Other contracts in 1997 were with American Express for $26 million and Rolex for $7.7 million. There was also a book contract for $2.2 million and articles in *Golf Digest*. In 1998, Tiger would add another $5 million to his earnings by making a video golf game for Entertainment Arts starring none other than Tiger Woods.

After his announcement in August 1996, Tiger would enter seven tournaments until the end of the year. His first tournament as a professional was in the Greater Milwaukee Open. He was outfitted in Nike clothes and bags while using Titleist clubs, balls, and glove. He felt like a kid at Christmas. Earl and Tida also wore Nike clothing. Tiger would become a walking advertisement for these companies. In 1997, Nike would recover their $40 million investment by selling Tiger's new clothing line to young people who wanted to wear what he wore.

Tiger made a poor beginning in Wisconsin. He tied for 60th, but he won $2,544. At the Canadian Open he tied for 11th, winning $37,500. In the Quad City Classic in Illinois he tied for 5th and won $42,150. At the B.C. Open in Endicott, New York, he crept up to a tie for 3rd and a win of $58,000.

Exhausted, Tiger arrived in Pine Mountain, Georgia, for the Buick Challenge. He withdrew after a practice round and flew back to his new home—a townhouse in Orlando, Florida. Behind him, a political storm erupted. A dinner had been arranged in Tiger's honor to award him a trophy that had been compared with the Heisman trophy. Buick had paid $30,000 for the dinner with about 200 people who had planned to attend. The players, the sponsor, and the guests were enraged when Tiger didn't show up.

Tiger's immaturity and poor judgment in withdrawing had tripped him. His regrets and apologies came too late. After media criticism, he wrote a letter of apology to each guest at the dinner. This was a hard lesson for the young man. But he requested that the dinner be rescheduled. The event took place in November, and again Tiger expressed his sincere regrets for his actions.

Next, Tiger entered the Las Vegas Invitational. Still suffering from the public criticism of the Buick Challenge, Tiger made a spectacular win for a prize of $297,000. These winnings already guaranteed his exemption from paying entry fees for the 1996, 1997, and 1998 PGA Tour. He made third place at the LaCantera Texas Open for $81,600 and he won the Walt Disney World/Oldsmobile Classic, spinning his earnings even higher to $216,000.

What happened next in Tulsa, Oklahoma, would disturb Tiger more than anything else in his life. He and his parents had gone to Tulsa for the PGA Tour championship. On the second round of the tournament, his father was rushed to the hospital with chest pains. Ten years before, Earl had had heart surgery. Tiger was desperately worried. He played an admirable round of golf and then dashed to his father's bedside. Tiger tied for 21st and then flew his parents home in a chartered jet. Nothing and no one was more important than his father.

Tiger would finish the year by tying for fifth at the Australian Open for a prize of $195,000. The biggest prize of all was to be named Rookie of the Year after only four months of playing golf as a professional. All this at twenty years of age.

In addition to his earnings, Tiger had many expenses. He had to pay his caddie ten percent of his earnings at each tournament. His agent, too, got a percentage of the contracts. Travel, hotels, and food would add to the tab. His father would become chairman of the ETW (Earl and Tiger Woods Foundation, Inc.) and receive a salary. This foundation would sponsor golf clinics for inner-city kids.

For the first time in his life, Tiger would be able to spend money on large items. Tiger was advised to avoid the high state income and sales taxes of California by moving to Florida. Florida has no state income tax. Many highly paid sports figures live in Florida for that reason.

Years ago, Arnold Palmer had bought two properties

northwest of Orlando in Windemere. Here he built two golf courses. One was the gray and white Bay Hill Country Club. Around the corner was the second one— Isleworth Country Club. The clubs are walled and private, and only expensive homes were built inside the walls and around the courses.

Orlando, Florida, has a certain charm. A six-lane highway curves through the heart of the city, dividing the lakes on either side. Chunky buildings and pastel towers house the mirrored glass offices. Disney World draws millions of tourists to its playground acres on Orlando's western flank. But golf is as big as Disney World in Florida.

Tiger Woods would become neighbor to golfer Mark O'Meara, baseball great Ken Griffey, Jr., actor Wesley Snipes, and others at Isleworth Country Club. Isleworth is in a remote area of Windemere, surrounded by a chain of lakes and abundant orange groves. Ivy vines are draped over the thick pink stucco walls around the complex. A guardhouse monitors the comings and goings of residents and visitors.

Tiger would find privacy behind the cloistered walls of Isleworth. In 1996 he purchased a half-million dollar townhouse there. Later, in 1997, he would spend $3 million for another two pieces of land on Lake Bessie to build his dream house eventually and his own nine holes. These purchases would also help lower his taxes on the mounting millions he was making.

It was fun living at Isleworth. He had his own golf cart

with a CD installed to play R & B (Rhythm and Blues), Jock James, and Montell Jordan's hip-hop music. Titleist supplied him with 2,000 balls every six months for practice and playing. After he practiced on the driving range, these balls would be separated and returned to the veranda of his house. Life in Isleworth was not like that in Cypress.

For relaxation Tiger would watch cartoons and movies or drive over to the Golf Channel offices. There, in the low modern buildings tucked away in an industrial park, Tiger would watch historic golf tapes in a special screening room. Or, Golf Channel host Peter Kessler might interview him. Other times Tiger would go fishing with Mark O'Meara or visit his friends and their families.

Tiger's rising star would have a bumpy ride in 1997. The first half of the year was up and the second half was down. He entered 21 of the 44 PGA tournaments. He found that golfing for ten months was much more strenuous than just for summers and occasional college tournaments. During this time, his parents would separate, but not divorce. Tida lived in a large home bought for her by Tiger in Tustin, California, not far from Cypress. Earl continued to live in the Cypress house. The parents appeared together at tournaments and were happy with this arrangement.

Before the Masters in April, Tiger played in eight tournaments. He kicked off the year by winning the Mercedes Championship, $216,000, and a Mercedes car. He would also buy a one-eighth interest ($1.9 million) in an executive jet, seating ten passengers, available for use at any time, and buy himself a Ford Expedition.

Once he captured the Masters prize and his green jacket, he rocketed into the hearts of American people. They loved the bashful grin and toothy smile from the 6-foot 2-inch slender young man. He cracked the racial barriers for minorities and African Americans who have long considered golf a sport for rich whites. But with fame also came many threats of a racist nature. Tiger had to hire a corps of bodyguards to protect him at tournaments. Even the pushing of fans almost injured his eye. Because of that, he had to change his patterns of life.

Tiger would capture four majors in 1997: the Mercedes; the Masters; the GTE Byron Nelson Classic in Irving, Texas; and the Motorola Western Open in Lemont, Illinois. By the year's end, Tiger would be number one in golf earnings—the first golfer to go over $2 million ($2,066,833), except for Hale Irwin on the senior tour, in a year. He would be selected to play on the Ryder Cup team to represent his country against European golfers. His teammates became friends instead of competitors that week in Spain.. He was also named PGA Player of the Year, Sportsman of the Year, Sports Star of the Year, ABC's Wide World of Sports Athlete of the Year, ESPN's Newsmaker of the Year, Associated Press's Male Athlete of the Year, and MSNBC's Person of the Year. The young golfer was considered one of the most polished and gracious sports celebrities of the year.

In a reflective mood about 1997, Tiger told the *Houston Chronicle* that it had taken him time to get used to the media and the pack of fans following him. The fans also were writing 4,000 letters a week to him while his agent received over 1,500 media requests a week. Whatever failures he had on the golf course were considered learning experiences for him. "When people wake up in the morning on the wrong side of the bed and they're in a grumpy mood and just unhappy with life, they can go out and say things and be okay with it. Unfortunately, I can't do that. I can't afford to have those kinds of days in public; and that's been one of the things hard to handle."

He continued: "I try and do my part to try and help those kids and sign autographs. But people fail to realize that I'm trying to get ready for a tournament. And when you're working on the range or on the putting green or on the golf course, it's very difficult when people are screaming and yelling for an autograph and stuff. Sometimes people lose sight of that."

Tiger's most prized moments on the golf course were in January, 1998 at the Pro-Am AT&T Tournament at Pebble Beach, California. Here he played with his father as his partner. In a Pro-Am (professional-amateur) an amateur golfer can pay as much as $5,000 to play with a professional. Much of the money goes to charity. Tiger and Earl did not play that well, but they had fun together.

As 1998 began, expectations were very high for Tiger.

These he discounted. His own expectations for himself were more important He knew the public can be very changeable in their likes and dislikes. They might like him one year and not the next year. Fame comes and goes. But Tiger's love of golf is unchangeable. He did tie for second in the Mercedes Championship with his friend, Mark O'Meara. At the Johnnie Walker Classic in Thailand, he came from way behind to beat Ernie Els of South Africa in a sudden death two-round play-off. His game became more consistent. He was placing second and third. But at the Bay Hill tournament in March, he slipped badly to 35th.

By the time April of 1998 arrived, Tiger was prepared to defend his title at the Masters. His coach, Butch Harmon, had flown in from Las Vegas to help him refine his swing and his game. But weather would challenge the golfers at Augusta. Tornadoes ripped through Alabama and Georgia. Torrential rains with thunder and lightning drenched the Masters course. Despite sunshine Thursday and Friday, the winds were gusty and lifted sand from the bunkers in sheets, throwing the grains into the eyes of the players and spectators. The golfers were fighting the winds to stay at even par. Scores were not spectacular.

Tiger was paired with the national Amateur champion, 19-year-old Matt Kuchar from Georgia Tech. Kuchar received more applause and cheers in his opening drive than Tiger. Easter Sunday would disappoint Tiger with a three-under-par score, tying him for eighth place. His good friend and neighbor, 41-year-old Mark O'Meara, would win the Masters for 1998 at nine under par. Tiger hugged him and fitted the green jacket on him. Although Tiger had lost, his hopes for every Masters will be to win.

Tiger's golf game was fairly steady throughout the 20 tournaments he entered in 1998. The beauty of his classic swing did not change. But his short game and putting were not as consistent or accurate as in 1997. Although he didn't win a major tournament, except the Johnnie Walker Classic in Thailand, the BellSouth Classic, and the PGA Grand Slam of Golf in Hawaii, he placed in the top ten 13 times. David Duval had the lowest scoring average for 1998 and Tiger was a close second. Tiger's earnings also stayed in the top ten of world players, and he remained ranked number one in the world. However, to repeat his spectacular performance of 1997 was a hard task.

In December of 1998 Tiger fulfilled a dream by meeting President Nelson Mandela of South Africa before playing a tournament there. Mandela handed Tiger a copy of his autobiography, *Long Walk to Freedom*, and told the media, "It's a great honor not only to me but also to South Africa that we have been visited by such a prominent sportsman."

Tiger tied for first in the million dollar South African tournament, but after a five-hole playoff, he placed second to Nick Price. Tiger, however, was mobbed at every hole by admiring fans.

The start of the 1999 PGA Tour had some roller-coaster rides for Tiger. Not until the Buick Invitational at the Torrey Pines Golf Course in San Diego, California, on Valentine's Day weekend did Tiger have a clear spectacular win. He made a course record of 62 one day and 22 under par for the tournament. It was also a sentimental win. At that course, he had won his sixth Junior amateur title. Tiger had not had a win since May of 1998 at the BellSouth Classic. The drought of losing 14 tournaments was over.

Another surprise for Tiger fans came in early March of 1999 when Tiger and his caddie of two and a half years, "Fluff" Mike Cowan, parted ways. Tiger decided to try New Zealander, Steve Williams, who had caddied for Raymond Floyd.

After The Player's Championship at Ponte Vedra, Florida, near Jacksonville, in March 1999, Tiger lost his number one ranking in the world to David Duval, who was on a winning streak.

Under the fickle skies and temperamental winds at the 1999 Masters tournament, Tiger Woods was not able to recapture the magic of his 1997 win. Woods and David Duval were expected to be the frontrunners of the tournament. They were not. Jose Maria Olazabal of Spain snatched victory away from Greg Norman and Davis Love III. Tiger would make one-over-par, landing him in a 5-way-tie for 8th place.

Not until late May of 1999 did Tiger break a three month dry period to win the Deutsche Bank Open in

Heidelberg, Germany. He was offered a million dollars for his appearance and then made a spectacular win of 15 under par and a score of 273 over four days. It was his first entry into the European Tour, and he won $200,000 as well.

After the European victory, Tiger regained his confidence. When he entered the Memorial Tournament in Dublin, Ohio, Tiger took the lead on the first day in early June 1999 and each of the four days thereafter, edging out Vijay Singh. He made some spectacular chip shots and putts for a win of $459,000, giving Tiger his second PGA Tour victory in the first half of 1999.

Although Tiger placed third in the U.S. Open in June of 1999, he streaked to victory at the Motorola Western Open over the July 4th weekend. With a 15-under par and winnings of $450,000, Tiger regained his number one ranking in the world. Only halfway through the year, Tiger had earned over $2.5 million.

Surging with confidence, Tiger arrived in Scotland for the British Open in mid-July to play at Carnoustie golf course. But the temperamental winds, knee-high grasses of the rough, and his own poor putting placed him seventh in the finish, but adding another $82,000 to his winnings. Despite his bitter disappointment at the loss, Tiger displayed enormous grace in defeat.

On August 2, 1999, Tiger and David Duval, the top two players on the PGA Tour, met for a duel on prime time television. They played 18 holes at the Sherwood

Country Club in Thousand Oaks, California to determine who was the best golfer. Against glaring lights and giant shadows on the fairways and greens, Tiger triumphed over Duval, winning a cool $1.1 million for the victory. Duval won $400,000, and they each donated $200,000 to charity from their winnings.

In mid-August, Tiger captured his second major championship since winning the Masters. At age 23 he was the youngest player to achieve that distinction. Tiger squeaked past nineteen-year-old Spanish sensation, Sergio Garcia, by one stroke to win the PGA Championship in Medinah, Illinois. His share of the winnings totaled $630,000. Woods and Garcia may well become the hot rivals in professional golf for the start of the 21st century.

Later in August, Tiger delivered a knockout-putt at the NEC Invitational to win the World Golf Championship at the Firestone Country Club in Akron, Ohio. With this victory he pocketed $1 million, pushing his earnings to well over $4 million. He also signed a five-year, $90 million deal with Nike to endorse their products. And at the 1999 Ryder Cup in Brookline, Massachusetts, Tiger and his American teammates squeezed victory away from the European team on the final sun-drenched day in late September.

Tiger's sixth victory of the year came at the Disney World National Classic over the Columbus Day weekend, sending his earnings to over $4.7 million. In late

October, and on the eve of the PGA Tour Championship in Houston, Texas, the golf world was dealt a crushing blow with the death of golf-great Payne Stewart in a tragic plane crash. Before play began, all the golfers went to Stewart's memorial service in Orlando, Florida. Once the tournament began, Tiger broke ahead of the pack to win his seventh victory and pocket $900,000 to hike his 1999 earning to over $5.6 million.

The 1999 season wound down with the American Express Championship in Spain at the Valderama Golf Club. Although Tiger lagged behind in the first couple of days, he clawed his way to a one-hole play-off to win his eighth victory of the year. With the $1 million purse, Tiger won the title "The Six Million Dollar Man for 1999." But he reached over seven million dollars in earnings by winning the World Cup in Malaysia and the PGA Grand Slam of Golf in Hawaii by year's end.

For the 23-year-old golf genius, the millennium count down broke some records for him. Not since 1953 had anyone topped Ben Hogan's four straight wins—until Tiger. Not since 1974 had anyone broken Johnny Miller's eight victories on the PGA Tour—until Tiger. The record Tiger still needs to beat is Byron Nelson's eleven consecutive wins in 1945, and he appears well on the way to doing it.

* * *

What does the future hold for Tiger Woods? He may marry and have a family. But he will continue to play golf to win—even when he loses. His goals are private ones that he will not share with anyone. As he told Golf Channel host Peter Kessler in a TV interview at the end of 1996, "My Dad told me that all he wanted for me was to be happy and be honest."

During Tiger's future golfing years, he probably will have dry periods and winning streaks. But his impact on the game has been far-reaching. Professionals and amateurs alike have worked harder on their games, raising the standard of playing. Fathers and children have become closer as fathers nurture the sports talents in their sons and daughters. Mothers have demanded better performance from their sons and daughters in school.

Butch Harmon, Tiger's coach, said in an interview at the 1998 Masters, "The beautiful thing about Tiger's talent is that he has brought kids of all nationalities to the game of golf."

Tiger has repeatedly said that he wants to be the best golfer in the world. Only time will tell if this goal can be fulfilled. Meanwhile, his performance on the PGA Tour will be carefully watched.

GLOSSARY

birdie—A hole scored in one stroke less than par.

bogey—A hole scored in one stroke over par.

bunker—A large sand trap on the golf course, especially near the greens.

chip—To make a short shot from about 20 yards away from the green that lofts the ball onto the green and allows it to roll.

divot—A lump of grass or dirt scooped up by a player's club when the ball is hit. Players must always put the divot back in the ground.

double-bogey—A hole played in two strokes over par.

drive—The act of hitting the ball from the tee as far as possible down the fairway.

eagle—A hole played in two strokes less than par on a par four or par five hole.

fairway—A mowed, grassy highway to the green, sometimes straight, but usually bending.

green—A carefully mowed area around the flag and cup for putting.

grip—The placing of the two hands on the club, either overlapping, interlocking, or in a baseball grip.

hook—To hit the ball with a right-to-left spin or left-to-right spin.

lie—The position in which the ball finally rests after being hit.

par—The standard number of strokes needed for each

hole. A par 3 is a hole up to 250 yards; a par four is between 251 and 470 yards; a par 5 is any hole longer than 470 yards.

pitch—To lob or lift the ball into a high arc so that it rolls very little after landing on the green.

putt—A stroke on the green intended to make the ball reach and drop into the cup.

rough—The part of the course that is not the fairway, tee, or green. It is the long grass.

short game—Chipping and pitching close to the green and putting into the cup with the fewest number of strokes.

sand trap—A sandy bunker called a hazard, from which it is difficult to chip out.

tee—A wooden peg or the space between two markers where the first drive is made on each hole.

Acknowledgments

Throughout the research for this book, I have been grateful to numerous people and institutions for their willingness to cooperate. The list includes: Stanford University; Wally Goodwin; Wiley and Janet Greig; Don Crosby; Corina Durrego; Carl Vanderbosch; Rudy Duran; Tom Sargent; John Anselmo; Wells Marvin; Butch Harmon; Mark Smith; Jack and Sandra Kamrath; Dick Harmon; PGA Tour offices; Golf Channel in Orlando; Shirley Steele; David and Roseanne Steele; the Farrells; Lucy Kabakian; Donna Musgrave; Paul Brown; Frank Young; Clare Rowland; Judy Tilley; Don Thomas; Sally Gessford.

Bibliography

Books

Roberts, Clifford. *The Story of the Augusta National Golf Club.* New York: Doubleday, 1976.

Rosaforte, Tim. *Tiger Woods.* New York: St. Martin's Press, 1997.

Sports Illustrated. *Tiger Woods.* New York: Fireside, 1997.

Strege, John. *Tiger.* New York: Broadway Books, 1997.

Woods, Earl. *Training a Tiger.* New York: Harper Collins, 1997.

Multimedia

Barbara Walters ABC television interview with Tiger Woods, 1997.

Charlie Rose PBS television interview with Earl Woods, May 7, 1997.

Highlights of 1997 Masters. Produced by Augusta National Golf Club, Inc.

Oprah Winfrey Show. Interview with Tiger and Earl Woods, April 24, 1997.

Peter Kessler interview with Tiger on the Golf Channel, December 18, 1996.

Tiger's Website, www.tigerwoods.com

CBS sportsonline.com

Magazines and Newspapers

Boston Globe, April 8-13, 1997.

Cape Cod Times, 1997, 1998, 1999.

The Christian Science Monitor, 1997, 1998, 1999.

The Desert Sun, April 9, 1997; August 26, 1997; October 7, 15, 29, 30, 31, 1997; Nov. 3, 25, 29, 30, 1997; Dec.1, 1997; April 9, 1998.

Golf Digest, August 1997.

Golf magazine, December 1997.

The Houston Chronicle, November 1, 1997; April 5, 1998.

Palm Springs Life, November 1997.

People magazine, June 16, 1997.

Time magazine, April 21, 1997; May 5, 1997; August 18, 1997

USA Today, October 29, 1997.